rubber duckie

It floats!

by Jodie Davis

RUNNING PRESS
PHILADELPHIA · LONDON

9 8 7 6 5 4 3 2 1
Digit on the right indicates the number of this printing

Library of Congress Control Number: 2003097392

ISBN 0-7624-1836-2

Cover, interior, and package design by Corinda Cook
Edited by Elizabeth Encarnacion
Photography by Gilbert King
Additional photo credits:
 ©2001 Sesame Workshop. "Sesame Workshop" and its logo are trademarks of Sesame Workshop.
  All rights reserved. Photographs by Richard Termine and Eduardo Patino: pp. 33, 36
 AFP Photo Roslan Rahman: p. 59
 Courtesy of Ann Ennis: p. 60

This book may be ordered by mail from the publisher.
Please include $2.50 for postage and handling.
But try your bookstore first!

Running Press Book Publishers
125 South Twenty-second Street
Philadelphia, Pennsylvania 19103-4399

Visit us on the web!
www.runningpress.com

Dedication

To rubber ducks in all shapes and sizes: thank you for filling our hearts with your sunshine and reassuring us that this is, in fact, a good, rubber duckie-like world!

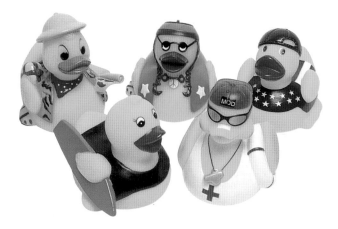

Special Thanks

To Craig Wolfe of Celebriducks, for championing me through this long process. The Dallas Cowboy cheerleaders could learn a lot from you!

To Mark Boldt, creator of Rubba Ducks, for your "giddy-up" rubber duck–like enthusiasm.

To Charlotte Lee, keeper of Duckplanet.com, for collecting and connecting all of us rubber duck lovers.

To my editor, Liz Encarnacion, for shining the literary limelight on the most deserving of subjects.

To Henri Herbert and Susan Cingari, for taking a chance on a woman in a bubble bath.

To eBay, for the steady wave of boxes of sunshine arriving at my door.

Table of Contents

Intro**duck**tion

From Childhood Icon to Hot Collectible

Rubber Duckie, you're the one. And these days, you're making more than just bath time lots of fun! Rubber duckies, those comforting companions from childhood bubble baths, are flocking back into the public eye. No longer restricted to their natural habitat, rubber duckies are a bona fide pop-culture phenomenon among sentimental adults, who are making the cute creatures the latest collecting craze, on par with Beanie Babies and Bobble Heads.

MVP: Most Valuable Plumage

As of this writing, the highest price paid at auction for a rubber duckie was $212.50 for a limited edition Alan Iverson Celebriduck on eBay.

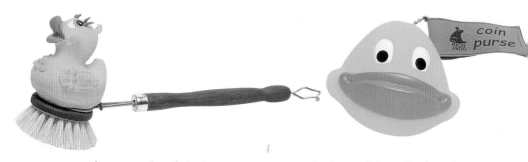

As a result of their resurgent popularity, rubber duckies have waddled out of the tub and onto everything from shower curtains to sterling-silver baby rattles. Wander into any department store, from Target to Neiman Marcus, and head to the bed and bath section. You'll find a world of rubber duckie items, including soap dishes and dispensers, bathmats and toothbrushes—even rubber-duckie clocks to count those bubbly fun minutes you spend in the bathtub with your fowl friends. With characteristic nostalgia, baby boomers are harkening back to pure, clean fun in the form of this childhood icon.

As rubber duckies make a huge splash in the world of merchandising and collecting, advertisers are starting to catch on. Companies like Mercedes-Benz and United Airlines employ images of rubber ducks in ads to convey the message that their products and services share the inherent qualities of wholesomeness, tradition, and safety that the classic rubber duck embodies. Yes, even savvy, serious business types think these childhood bath toys are the paradigms of all that is good!

With rubber duckie products selling out at major retailers and everyone from Shakespeare to Snoop Dogg being depicted in rubber-duck form, it's clear that this trend is floating its way into the mainstream. So draw some water in your tub, add a generous helping of bubble bath, and treat yourself to a fun bathtime story!

Linnaean Classification

So where does our treasured friend fit into the biological scheme of things? According to Vicki Funk of the Smithsonian Natural History Museum, the rubber duck perches neatly on the Linnaean hierarchy of biological order as *annis* (duck) *plastica* (rubber) and is in the rubber tire genus. Naturally, rubber duckie is close kin to the rubber chicken, *Gallus heavia*.

Rubber Duckie
through the Years

"Early on, we tried to do a little genealogical research on the rubber duck. He turned out to be surprisingly elusive. We tracked him back a couple of generations to the World War II era and then found a few earlier references to his cousin, the celluloid duck. (The latter apparently had literary aspirations; he's mentioned in both D.H. Lawrence's *Lady Chatterley's Lover* and Dylan Thomas's *A Child's Christmas in Wales*.) Finally, we found a very early magazine article, 1869 to be exact, that referred to 'Foster's India-Rubber Duck.' The great-granddaddy of the rubber duck? Alas, a closer reading showed that Foster's was an India rubber *decoy* duck—the black sheep of the family!"

—Ellen Pawelczak, Rich Frog Industries

Early Origins

How did the rubber duckie originate? Was it a child's fantasy? A toy manufacturer's marketing success? A sudden moment of divine enlightenment?

Ever the enigmatic figure, rubber duckie's childhood years are shrouded in mystery. No patent exists for a first, defining rubber duck. No rags-to-riches toymaker fairytale resides in entrepreneurial chronicles, nor a Raggedy Ann–like character in a children's book to inspire the toys.

The simple truth appears to be that the birth of the rubber duckie was a progression born of children's affection for baby animals, brought to play in the bath in the most appropriate material—rubber—and the most aquatically inclined little animal, the duck.

On his fourth voyage to the New World, in 1503, Christopher Columbus and his crew were astonished to see the natives bouncing a heavy black ball. The buoyant characteristic of the vegetable gum now known as latex led them to describe the ball as being "alive." When the substance was found to rub out pencil marks, the English named it *rubber*.

The first rubber ducks were made entirely of dark, hard, solid rubber. Children enjoyed rubber ducks as early as the late nineteenth century, as evidenced by the following poem, published in the *Amador Dispatch* in California on August 25, 1899. However, those ducks were much different than the ones that swim in our bath tubs today.

The Old Rubber Duck By Joe Cone in Little Folks

The rubber duck whistles, the rubber duck squeaks,

The rubber duck listens and mutters and speaks

It jumps and it tumbles and oft has a fall,

But nothing can equal the old rubber duck.

A hundred times a day our little one kisses it

A hundred times a day our little one misses it

A hundred times a day our little one, she makes it squall

Then she catches it and blesses it.

And smoothes it and caresses it.

And talks very stern to her old rubber duck.

The rubber duck scolds, the rubber duck squeaks,

The rubber duck whispers and it cries, with a pitiful call.

But the baby just worships her old rubber duck.

A hundred times a day our little one sighs for it,

A hundred times a day, our little one cries it,

A hundred times a day she lets it fall

Then she catches it and snugs it up

And drowsily she hugs it up

And drops off to slumber with her old rubber duck.

Prior to World War II, rubber toys were made by compressing a chunk of uncured rubber stock in a mold. High temperatures and heavy pressure forced the rubber to conform to the mold cavity, with excess rubber squeezed out along the parting line at the junction of the two halves of the mold. This process accounts for the lines evident along the sides of some

rubber ducks, much like those on a chocolate Easter bunny. Because of the characteristics of natural rubber, these early dolls and toys succumbed to heat and coldness, becoming sticky in hot weather and losing elasticity in low temperatures.

New Materials Make Duckie Durable

A new day dawned for rubber toys when inventor Charles Goodyear accidentally overheated a mixture of sulfur, rubber, and white lead on a hot stove. He discovered vulcanization, a way to make a hard and durable substance that chars but does not melt. One of the first to apply Goodyear's patented process to rubber-toy making was Benjamin F. Lee, of the New York Rubber Company. Founded in 1851 on

Staten Island, the company made all-rubber, black or white boy and girl dolls dressed in knitted clothes. While more durable than their predecessors, these vulcanized rubber toys still deteriorated over time, making those found today in good condition highly collectible.

The evolution of duckies from rubber to plastic and vinyl started in 1939 when U.S. chemist Bradley Dewey opened a pilot plant for making synthetic rubber. In 1952 the Ohio company Auburn, manufacturer of toy soldiers and cars, started production with the first plastic-injection molding machine. Still

rubber-like, the toys no longer warped nor cracked. Most important, the new material allowed for higher quality in the sculpting and details.

During the post-war period, toy manufacturers retooled with the expensive steam-jacketed molding presses that had been so successfully used to produce war materials. On the heels of this investment, poly vinyl chloride (PVC) was developed by B.F. Goodrich and immediately outmoded this technology. With this innovation, high-volume production in the U.S. toy industry became a reality in the early 1950s. The Polymer Age had begun!

Rubber Duckie Pioneers

Between 1905 and 1955, millions upon millions of rubber toys were made in the Akron, Ohio area. In fact, during this period nearly one hundred companies were producing toys in Summit County.

Sun Rubber

Sun Rubber dominated the rubber toy industry for many years, churning out a flotilla of trucks, ships, and tanks in addition to rubber dolls and toys, footballs, basketballs, and Disney toys. In Joan Stryker Gubaugh's *A Collector's Guide to the Gerber Baby*, one of the designers of Sun Rubber's toys explained the technique used in that plant to make millions of toys.

According to Ed Mobley, early hollow dolls and toys were crafted by "blowing" thin sheets of soft and spongy uncured rubber against both halves of the mold. Sodium bicarbonate was placed between the two halves to force the rubber outward against the compression mold. Examples of Sun Rubber's superbly sculpted and detailed toys are easily obtained on eBay today.

Rempel Manufacturing

A true story of the American Dream, the history of Rempel Manufacturing also involves a fairy tale. Russian-born Dietrich Rempel arrived in the United States in 1922, penniless. At some point, he worked as a development engineer at Sun Rubber. In true entrepreneurial, there-must-be-a-better-way style, Rempel developed an innovative process to manufacture his latex toys, designed the machinery he needed, and started his own company. His system discarded the traditional steam and pressure molds and expensive rubber compounding machinery, making the process of manufacturing a rubber toy faster and cheaper.

Simplicity was inherent in the Rempel roto-cast process. To cast a toy, latex was poured into plaster molds, which were rotated on two different axes. After being cured in gas ovens for several hours, the toys were then hand painted with beautiful detail. In 1956 Rempel became the first toy firm to adopt urethane coating for its products. The transparent material gave the toys a high gloss finish and enabled them to be sterilized by dipping them into boiling water.

An accomplished sculptor, Rempel modeled in clay each of the fifty-one toys his company produced. Many of the animals were in the Little Folks from Sunny Slope line of rubber toys that appeared in *Deegie and the Fairy Princess*, a children's picture book illustrated by Rempel himself and written by his wife, Ruth. Based on his youth in Russia, the fairytale book is highly collectible today.

The last company in the nation to make rubber toys, Rempel merged with Blazon in 1966 and phased out squeak toys the following year.

"Duckie" or "Ducky?"

A critical question of great magnitude for all rubber duck lovers, the correct spelling of the name of their bath buddies is a subject often raised. It appears to be a matter of personal taste among rubber duck collectors. According to one online poll that has collected more than 2100 votes,

the two are running bill to bill, with 51 percent of respondents preferring "ducky" and 48 percent favoring "duckie" as of this printing. However, most compelling is the fact that *Sesame Street*'s Ernie, the undisputed number one fan of these yellow creatures, serenades his rubber duck*ie* in the official version of his signature song. Who can argue with the expert?

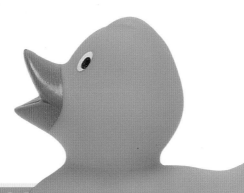

Sesame Street
Serenade

Admit it. Ever since you picked up this kit and started reading, you've had a certain song running through your head. Which one? *Sesame Street*'s "Rubber Duckie," of course!

It's the signature song of the Muppet Ernie, whose favorite pastime is taking a bubble bath with his rubber duckie while singing to him.

How did this facet of Ernie's personality come about? To answer this question we must step back in time to the earliest days of *Sesame Street*. The characters were being developed and the puppets designed; the format of the show, the music, and the set were all brainstormed, rehearsed, and perfected into a whole. As part of this flurry of creativity, Joe Raposso and Jeff Moss had quite a rivalry going while they created the songs that have since become classics. Joe wrote such favorites as "Sing" and "Being Green" while Jeff composed "People in Your Neighborhood," "I Love Trash," and our favorite, "Rubber Duckie."

Although the team usually worked by starting with the lyrics that existed in the show's script, then adding the music, "Rubber Duckie" originated from music and a discussion about children playing with a bath toy. The script was then written around the song. As for the titular fowl, it was simply a rubber duckie bought locally to play the part of Ernie's squeaking friend on screen.

Rubber Duckie

Rubber Duckie, you're the one,
You make bath time lots of fun,
Rubber Duckie, I'm awfully fond of you;
(yo yo, dee d)

Rubber Duckie, joy of joys,
When I squeeze you, you make noise,
Rubber Duckie, you're my very best friend, it's true.
(doo doo doo doooo, doo doo)

Oh, every day when I,
Make my way to the tubby
I find a little fellow who's
Cute and yellow and chubby!
(Rub-a-dub-a-dub-by!)

Rubber Duckie, you're so fine.
And I'm lucky that you're mine
Rubber duckie, I'm awfully fond of you!

Every day when I
Make my way to the tubby
I find a little fellow who's
Cute and yellow and chubby!
(Rub-a-dub-a-dub-by!)

Rubber Duckie, you're so fine.
And I'm lucky that you're mine
Rubber duckie, I'm awfully fond of you!

Sung by Ernie (Jim Henson)

Words & Music by Jeff Moss

The song became so hot that the folks at *Sesame Street* fielded a flood of requests for sheet music and tapes. "Rubber Duckie" became a pop culture phenomenon and was recorded in some seventy languages. A German compact disc featuring five different versions of the song, including a dance remix, sold nearly two million copies!

In the early seventies, the *Sesame Street* cast was invited to join the Boston Pops, with Arthur Fiedler as conductor, for a concert of all the *Sesame Street* classics. During rehearsals, composer Jeff Moss marched in with a box of one hundred rubber duckies, one for each of the members of the orchestra to squeak at the end of every stanza of "Rubber Duckie." A meeting of the orchestra committee was called immediately. The issue: this was considered "doubling" under the musician union's rules—squeaking the rubber ducks would make them a second instrument, requiring extra

pay! Eventually it was agreed that as musical instruments, rubber ducks would fall into the percussion category, and would thereby not require a doubling of pay if squeaked by that section of the orchestra alone!

Ernie revisited his love of rubber duckies with an all-star cast in *Put Down the Duckie*, available on video and DVD. True to form, Ernie has a bit of a problem in his attempts to play his instrument and requests assistance from an expert, a saxophone playing owl who advises him that he'll need to put down the duckie. Stay tuned when the credits roll; the encore versions with Barbara Walters, Paul Simon, Danny DeVito, and other stars singing and dancing will have you singing along!

His Royal Duckiness

Rubber duckies have fans even among the highest ranks of society. A rubber duck sporting an inflatable crown was spotted by a decorator as he was refurbishing the Buckingham Palace living quarters of Queen Elizabeth II in 2001. In a screaming headline blazoned across the front page of Britain's *Sun* tabloid, the decorator was reported as saying, "I was repainting the Queen's bathroom walls in the same colour she's had for the last 50 years when I glanced down at the bath.... I nearly fell off my step ladder when I saw a yellow rubber duck with an inflatable crown on its head." He presumed that the Queen's grandchildren had given it to her as a joke, but only the dignified duckie knows for sure.

The Modern Duckie
Field Guide

Like their predecessors, today's rubber duck makers are quite an inspired bunch. And what a cast of characters they produce! The Goodview Industries line includes baseball players, hippies, a bird watcher, and a hilarious stock broker duck carrying money and talking on a cell phone. Among Assurance Industry's on-growing collection of ducksonalities is a chef toting a spoon and wearing the appropriate jacket and popover hat, a sheriff with cowboy hat, a floating space shuttle duck, a firefighter, and football player and cheerleader ducks. Fun in the sun is on tap for Beachline's duck, who relaxes in a striped inner

41

tube with sunglasses perched at the top of his head. Joanne Cassaro produces mod rubber ducks such as a brawny lifeguard duck and a leather clad biker duck. Rubber ducks are even sports fans, uniformed by Strike Zone for everyone's favorite baseball teams.

The debut of the red devil duck, with his black horns and not so traditional facial expression, caused quite a stir in the rubber duck collecting world. Quickly following up with green, blue, pink, and violet versions, manufacturer Accoutrements has also added metallic gold and silver devil ducks, polka dot and glow-in-the-dark ducks, and smaller versions that include key chains.

The First Years

Picture the ubiquitous rubber duck found in grocery stores everywhere, the one that comes to mind when one hears the words "rubber duck." That's one of the ducks made by The First Years, who started selling ducks fifty-two years ago, and commenced manufacturing their proprietary line in 1972. All in all, the company has sold more than 7,150,000 rubber ducks over the past ten years!

Rubba Ducks

Rubba Ducks certainly have personality! Their creator, entrepreneur Mark Boldt, designs his ducks with the philosophy that every child belongs and, like every duck, every child is unique and special. So, as the Rubba Ducks song goes, "They're a lot like U and a lot like me."

Each Rubba Duck character is produced as a limited edition, and includes a tattoo reflecting its individuality, a biography, a trading card hang tag, and a hatch date. Count Duckula wears the requisite cape, is tattooed with a bat, and comes packaged with the saying, "I've come to swim in your suds." Attired appropriately in a ten gallon hat and a bandana, pinto-spotted Cowduck "would rather be home on the range." And Duckerina, with her toe shoes tattoo declares, "Ballet . . . it's the love of the dance, the shoes, and of course my pink tutu."

Rubba Ducks are introduced in "waves" of limited editions which "migrate" (retire) to make room for new ducks, turning the retired ducks into immediate collectibles. Of course, the appeal of Rubba Ducks isn't limited to the young, for as Boldt asserts, "Every child under the age of 112 can identify with them! Isn't it time you got in touch with your inner duck?"

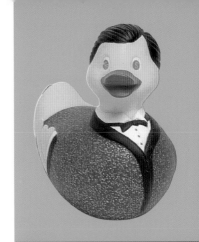

Celebriducks

"Rub-a-dub with stars in your tub." For Celebriducks creator Craig Wolfe, what started as a wacky idea from a friend has turned into a multi-million dollar corporation. The concept? Putting the likenesses of celebrities on rubber ducks. Wolfe and his duck-designing daughter Rebecca began their venture by immortalizing the likes of Betty Boop, William Shakespeare, Santa Claus, James Brown, the Mona Lisa, and even Queen Elizabeth I in the form of carefully detailed bath time buddies. Striking a chord for their humorous portrayals, Celebriducks quickly attracted a cult following. But their big break came from another arena of celebridom: sports.

Included on *Entertainment Weekly*'s list of the Top 100 gifts of 2001, Celebriducks attracted the attention of the NBA's Philadelphia 76ers, who ordered 5,000 Allen Iverson Celebriducks to be given away as a promotion at a 76ers game. Complete with cornrows and tattoos, this daring duck pleased the celebrity himself and brought NASCAR, the NHL, and MLB speeding, cross-checking, and dribbling to Wolfe's door. It's no wonder Celebriducks is often mentioned as the next great collecting fad for former fans of Beanie Babies and Bobbleheads.

"Let My Duckies Go!"

Finding himself laid off from a Judaic software company, Benjamin Goldman of Chicago decided to marry his interest in sports with his religious beliefs by commissioning his own branded series of ducks from Celebriducks. The first, a limited edition of 2,500 based on Michelangelo's *Moses in Chains*, debuted in 2003 exclusively on eBay and portrays Moses holding the Ten Commandments.

Rich Frog Industries

Not long after Rich Frog Industries, a Vermont-based children's toy and gift company, was founded, the Original Rubber Duck waddled into our lives. People just could not get enough of this slightly goofy-looking little character from Spain, and he soon became—and remains—one of their biggest sellers. As part of their line of classic bath toys, Rich Frog now offers a whole range of rubber ducks, but it's the Original who's still "tops of the bill."

"We get lots of letters from our rubber-duck fans, but one in particular stands out. After purchasing a Rich Frog *Original Rubber Duck*, a customer discovered the following care label had been inadvertently affixed to the box: 'After washing, brush gently to restore the plush.' She duly wrote us. Was it a mistake, she asked——or had her duck's hair fallen out due to the trauma of transit? Should she take him to a duck psychologist for therapy? Our rubber-duck specialist wrote back: 'After consulting with several prominent duckologists (rest assured, none of them were quacks), we have determined that your *Original Rubber Duck* is most likely suffering from a mild case of mistaken identity, no doubt due to an unfortunate case of juvenile mislabeling. We would like to assure you that his condition is not serious. We suggest gently reassuring your duck that he does not need his plush restored and is not suffering from any form of mallard pattern baldness. He can stand proud in the knowledge that he is an *Original Rubber Duck* and, as such, cannot possibly be improved on.' (We believe he fully recovered.)"

—Ellen Pawelczak, Rich Frog Industries

Making a Duck Float Upright

Have you noticed that some of your rubber ducks find it difficult to swim without rolling on their sides? So did at least two modern-day rubber duck makers, causing them to insist that their ducks float heads up. But what sounded like a simple requirement turned into a major feat. Craig Wolfe of Celebriducks spent two years perfecting rubber duck aquatics. "Apparently no one we spoke with in China knew how to make a Celebriduck float properly," he says. Eventually Wolfe teamed with Assurance Industries, specialists in rubber duck engineering and manufacturing, who figured out how to make a duck swim with his head out of the water.

Rubber Duckies
on the Move

Swimming to the Aid of Science

Oceanographers are learning a lot from rubber duckies these days. In January of 1992 a freighter set out from Hong Kong. A storm brewed up, washing twelve forty-foot containers that housed a total of 29,000 bath toys from the deck of the freighter into the ocean.

Competent swimmers, the duckies emerged from their packaging after a day or so and bobbed on the waves, carried by the wind and ocean currents. Oceanographers suddenly had—quite by accident—a dreamily large sample of toys released into the ocean that would follow ocean currents, giving scientists a better understanding of their patterns. Anticipating a rare opportunity to glean useful information, advertisements were placed in newspapers and lighthouse operators were notified to solicit reports of landings.

The ducks started appearing in the waters of Sitka, Alaska by Thanksgiving and soon found themselves lounging in beachcombers' hot tubs. Combining the reports with computer models, the researchers learned that the ducks had headed northeast across the Pacific from the location of the accident, some heading north toward the Bering Sea. More than ten years later, after an epic journey that likely included the toys hitchhiking on slow moving ice through the North Pole, computer projections and landing reports indicated that some of the ducks made it to the North Atlantic coast and Greenland with the hardiest of the flock continuing on to Great Britain and Africa!

Plotting out the landings has provided important information regarding the way in which winds and ocean currents affect one another. And with a rash of new sightings expected after the toys' Arctic adventure, the company who made the ducks is offering a reward for anyone who finds one of the ducks in New England, Canada, or Iceland to prove the scientists' predictions correct. Now, when more dangerous spills inevitably occur, the information revealed by the shipwrecked duckies will enable oceanographers to better predict the drift of the spilled materials, thereby aiding cleanup efforts.

Lucky Duck

Arriving at the 2001 Academy Awards with a pocketful of good luck charms, Russell Crowe was especially attached to a rubber duck given to him by Jodie Foster's son, Charlie, saying, "Actors are incredibly superstitious people." Apparently, the magical charm of the duck worked, as he departed with an Oscar for Best Actor in *Gladiator*.

Racing for Charity

The latest craze in the world of fund raising, rubber duck races have turned our squeaky friends into fiercely competitive athletes in a race for the finish line to raise considerable funds for charity. The brainchild of Eric Schechter, Great American Duck Races is the wackiest and fastest-growing fund-raising scheme in the nation. The company leases thousands of ducks to charities who ask participants to adopt each numbered duck for a sponsorship fee. With all the excitement of the Indianapolis 500, throngs cheer as a dump truck deposits its yellow cargo of quackers into a river, canal, or lake. Swimming at a top speed of nine miles per hour and taking anywhere from two minutes to an hour to complete the course, the ducks race down the waterway to the finish line, winning prizes for their adopters. But the real winners are the non-profit organizations who have raised hundreds of thousands of dollars thanks to our fearless and benevolent little friends.

It's a Bird, It's a Plane . . .
It's *Rubber Duckie?*

While driving home from a ballooning competition one day, Susan and Brian Owen came up with the idea of creating a 90-foot tall Rubber

Duckie balloon. Weighing 350 pounds when deflated, Rubber Duckie fits in a bag four-feet across and travels in the bed of their fifteen passenger van, with the basket secured on the tailgate. Much to their surprise, Rubber Duckie has proven to be even more popular than their previous balloons, and has been invited to such faraway locales as New Zealand and Australia.

All the Comforts of Home

The exceptional feelings evoked by rubber ducks have not gone unnoticed by hoteliers. At the W Hotel in New York, privileged guests sleep under goose down duvets and 200 thread count sheets—and they find a rubber duck in their bath room to greet them. Forget the M&M's and $5 bottled water . . . at the whimsical Hotel Triton, San Francisco's un-hotel, collectible rubber ducks are featured in each room's honor bar. Further down the coast, at The Georgian Hotel in Santa Monica, every evening at turndown a towel is folded to resemble a wave, placed on the edge of each suite's bathtub, and topped with a rubber duck. And these fowl experiences are not limited to the United States— rubber ducks are wading into bathrooms from Helsinki to Hong Kong to keep travelers company when they're far from home!

Technical Duck Descriptors

Often quacking to their own beat, rubber ducks don't always fall into the generic floating posture. To alleviate confusion, collector Charlotte Lee of Duckplanet.com has coined some descriptors to categorize those ducks that run afowl of tradition.

Floater: A rubber duck designed to float in water

Stander: A rubber duck designed to stand or sit upright on a hard surface

Piggyback Duck: **A rubber duck designed to carry just one smaller duck on its back**

Piggyback Duck Set: **A Piggyback Duck plus one duckling**

Cadillac Duck: **A raft-like duck designed to carry two or more ducks on its back**

Cadillac Duck Set: **A Cadillac duck plus ducklings**

Birds of a Feather
Flock Together

Rubber Duckie Collecting Tips

Now that you have one duckie (included in this kit) to entertain you in the tub, you're hooked. He'll look up at you with those cute, innocent eyes, and you'll know he wants a feathered friend to keep him company. Soon, like so many others, your collection will be growing at an exponential rate, and you'll be scouring gift shops and online auctions for your next big find. Welcome to rubber duckie fanaticism.

Here are a few tips to help you survive and thrive as you build a collection:

1. Decide whether you want your collection to have a specific theme.
Are you a purist who only wants traditional yellow duckies gracing your shelves? A sports fan who aims to collect a full roster of athlete look-alikes and rubber duckie giveaways from games? Or do you make a point of welcoming all duckies into your family, regardless of age, color, or design? Once you've decided how to structure your collection, you'll have a better idea of where to find new acquisitions.

2. Do your homework. Many rubber duckie collectors have created websites about their collections, including photographs of their ducks. They're a great way to see the incredible variety of duckies that are available, and the collectors are invariably happy to answer questions about where they found the ducks or how they manage their collections. These websites also often have recommendations of the best stores for finding quality ducks.

Collection Craziness

After twenty years of collecting, Roger Ellison of California has a grand total of 1127 rubber ducks and is hoping to make it into the Guinness Book of World Records for the largest rubber duckie collection. It all started in 1982 when Roger was given a rubber duck as a gag gift. Before long, his collection had out grown the bathroom and was waddling into the record books!

3. When buying a brand-new duckie, try to keep the box and tags intact. The new, character-driven ducks are being made in limited editions to increase their collectibility. Like any other collectible, a pristine duckie in its original packaging will be worth more money in the future than one that's seen a lot of use.

4. Yard sales and online auctions are good sources for old ducks. One person's trash is another's treasure, which is why rubber duckies are highly trafficked on eBay and other online auction sites. A duckie that a child has outgrown might also pop up in a toy box at a yard sale for a very reasonable price, and you may find other deals while you're at it!

5. Find an appropriate display area for your collection. Are your duckies in active service, living full time in the shower, or will they sit on a shelf in your bathroom, ready to dive into the tub at a moment's notice? Maybe they are true collectibles, packed away or carefully arranged in a special display in another room of your house. Wherever and however you keep your collection, make sure there's room to expand, as duckie flocks have a tendency to multiply like crazy!

6. Most important, have fun! After all, the reason you're collecting duckies instead of coins or stamps is probably because rubber duckies bring back fond memories. So don't let your collection get too serious—be willing to bring a few of your duckies into the tub for a nice, relaxing bubble bath every now and then!

Duckie Hygiene

Are your ducks exhibiting the effects of so many baths? Do you have an old duck a child loved a little too much? Here are some tips from rubber duck collectors that should send your rubber duckie cleaning woes down the drain.

• Avoid sun exposure.

• Do not store on varnished or lacquered shelves.

• After giving your duck a bath, be sure to dry him out well, especially if he squeaks or has a hole on the bottom. As with other bathtub accessories, mold and mildew can be a problem when water is allowed to stay inside.

• If improperly stored ducks become misshapen, immerse them in hot water or tumble them in the dryer. When exposed to heat, the vinyl will "remember" its original shape. Then "fix" it by dipping it in cold water.

- For long term storage, wrap your rubber duckies in acid-free tissue or a soft cloth to avoid distortion, and seal in clean polyethylene bags.

- For general cleaning, mildew, and stains, try Formula 409, Soft Scrub with bleach, or Oxyclean. Alcohol is not recommended for any painted toy as it can remove the paint.

- Banish cigarette and musty odors by soaking the duck in a bath of hot water and baking soda. For persistent odors, wrap the duck in a paper towel and place it on a layer of baking soda in a plastic container. Seal for about a week, then replace the baking soda and repeat until the smell is gone.

- To remove ink marks, coat the mark with Oxy-10 acne treatment and leave it on for ten days. It will dry to a white powder that you simply wash off. Or try Remove-Zit which is reported by Barbie collectors not to remove color from the vinyl.

Spending Quality Time
with Your Quacker

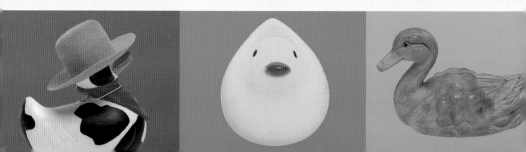

The Bubble Bath

The second most essential ingredient to bath time fun, bubbles trace their history at least as far back as the seventeenth century, as evidenced by Flemish paintings of the period that feature children blowing bubbles with clay pipes. Generations of eighteenth and nineteenth century mothers made use of their leftover washing soap by giving it to their children to blow bubbles. But bubbles didn't come into commerce until the beginning of the twentieth century, when street vendors began peddling bubbles as a toy. Then, in the early 1940s, the chemical company Chemtoy, which primarily sold cleaning supplies, revolutionized the toy world by bottling bubble solution for the first time. Tootsietoy Company soon acquired the

company and put bubble solution into full retail distribution in the late 1940s. Several decades later, bubble making companies like Imperial, Wells, and Pustifix came into being, increasing world-wide sales of bubble solution bottles to more than 200 million a year.

Make Your Own Bubble Bath

Have a rollicking good time in your tub with your duckie buddies using this homemade bubble bath recipe. It's easy! Although any soap can be used, Castile results in a superior bubble bath. Glycerin is the magic ingredient—approved by rubber duckies—that makes the bubbles. Both are known for their skin-softening qualities and can be found at health food stores.

1 quart water
1 bar (4 ounces) Castile soap
2 ounces glycerin
Essential oil (optional)

Mix the water and soap in a pot and cook over low heat, stirring occasionally, until the soap has dissolved. Pour the mixture into a bowl, add the glycerin, and mix. Slowly add drops of the essential oil, if desired, until the preferred scent is attained. Pour into jars and cap. To use, add about one cup of the solution to your tub as it fills.

In a perfect union of two of the world's most wonderful things, the Art CoCo Chocolate Company of Denver has created a yellow chocolate rubber duck. These lemon-flavored delights are formed of solid Guittard white chocolate and are hand-tinted to look almost identical to a real rubber duckie. Now you can nosh on your chocolate rubber duck before or after you join your ducks in a steaming bathtub!

World Wide
Webbed

Rubber duckie has certainly adapted to the technological age! With countless Web sites around the world dedicated to rubber duckie collections, products, games, and even a duckie Web cam, this is one fowl with a devoted following! We've provided a few of our favorite links, but please keep in mind that the Internet is constantly evolving, and some of the sites listed here may have migrated by the time you try them.

The Ultimate Rubber Duckie Web Site

Duckplanet.com has been providing information to online rubber duck fans since October of 2000. Launched simply as a means for Charlotte Lee to share her collection of more than 1,050 ducks with friends, family, and other duck-minded people, Duckplanet has become rubber duck central on the Internet. Check out the site to see Charlotte's extensive and well-documented collection, plus photos from collectors all over the world, updated sources and links, and a bubbling tub full of other features. It's a rubber duck lover's paradise! www.duckplanet.com

Online Duck Sources

These online stores specialize in unique rubber duck merchandise.

Captainquack.com

Celebriducks.com

Duckrace.com

eBay.com

Pricehot.com

Rubbaducks.com

Shadesplus.com

Zydecogifts.com

Duckie Web Cam

Check out this fun site for a voyeuristic look at a rubber duckie's busy day: duckcam.imbri.org/

Spell Check

Vote for your favorite spelling—Duckie or Ducky—at www.angelfire.com/retro/rubberducky/

About the Author

When she's not chin deep in bubbles and rubber ducks, Jodie Davis writes quilting and crafts books, numbering twenty-six to date, and is the host of the television show *Friends in the Bee*. She appeared with her duckie collection on A&E's *Incurable Collector*. Please visit her website at www.rubberduckie.net.